Nan's Secret Password Book: Protect Your Internet Usernames and Passwords

Dubreck World Publishing

Copyright

'Nan's Secret Password Book: Protect Your Internet Usernames and Passwords'

First published in July 2021 by Dubreck World Publishing
Printed and bound by Lulu Press
Distributed by Lulu Press

Copyright © 2021 Dubreck World Publishing, Hampshire, UK

All rights reserved. No part of this publication may be reproduced, stored in a retrieval system, or transmitted, in any form or by any means, without the prior permission in writing of the publisher, not be otherwise circulated in any form other than that in which it is published.

ISBN-13: 978-1-291-58885-9
First Edition

Disclaimer
Your password and any information you write in this book should be kept confidential. Keep this book in a safe and secure place. By using this book you acknowledge and agree that neither the publishers or authors of this book are in anyway liable or responsible for any damages resulting from the theft, loss or unauthorised use of your book and the information you place inside it.

DUBRECK WORLD PUBLISHING

For Nan

If found, please contact:	
Name:	
Phone:	
Email:	

Website	
Username	
Password	
Notes	

Website	
Username	
Password	
Notes	

Website	
Username	
Password	
Notes	

Website	
Username	
Password	
Notes	

Website	
Username	
Password	
Notes	

Website	
Username	
Password	
Notes	

Website	
Username	
Password	
Notes	

Website	
Username	
Password	
Notes	

Website	
Username	
Password	
Notes	

Website	
Username	
Password	
Notes	

Website	
Username	
Password	
Notes	

Website	
Username	
Password	
Notes	

Website	
Username	
Password	
Notes	

Website	
Username	
Password	
Notes	

Website	
Username	
Password	
Notes	

-B-

Website	
Username	
Password	
Notes	

Website	
Username	
Password	
Notes	

Website	
Username	
Password	
Notes	

-B-

Website	
Username	
Password	
Notes	

Website	
Username	
Password	
Notes	

Website	
Username	
Password	
Notes	

-B-

Website	
Username	
Password	
Notes	

Website	
Username	
Password	
Notes	

Website	
Username	
Password	
Notes	

-B-

Website	
Username	
Password	
Notes		

Website	
Username	
Password	
Notes		

Website	
Username	
Password	
Notes		

-B-

Website	
Username	
Password	
Notes	

Website	
Username	
Password	
Notes	

Website	
Username	
Password	
Notes	

Website	
Username	
Password	
Notes	

Website	
Username	
Password	
Notes	

Website	
Username	
Password	
Notes	

Website	
Username	
Password	
Notes	

Website	
Username	
Password	
Notes	

Website	
Username	
Password	
Notes	

Website	
Username	
Password	
Notes	

Website	
Username	
Password	
Notes	

Website	
Username	
Password	
Notes	

-C-

Website	
Username	
Password	
Notes	

Website	
Username	
Password	
Notes	

Website	
Username	
Password	
Notes	

Website	
Username	
Password	
Notes	

Website	
Username	
Password	
Notes	

Website	
Username	
Password	
Notes	

-D-

Website	
Username	
Password	
Notes	

Website	
Username	
Password	
Notes	

Website	
Username	
Password	
Notes	

Website	
Username	
Password	
Notes	

Website	
Username	
Password	
Notes	

Website	
Username	
Password	
Notes	

-D-

Website	
Username	
Password	
Notes	

Website	
Username	
Password	
Notes	

Website	
Username	
Password	
Notes	

Website	
Username	
Password	
Notes	
Website	
Username	
Password	
Notes	
Website	
Username	
Password	
Notes	

-D-

Website	
Username	
Password	
Notes	

Website	
Username	
Password	
Notes	

Website	
Username	
Password	
Notes	

Website	
Username	
Password	
Notes	

Website	
Username	
Password	
Notes	

Website	
Username	
Password	
Notes	

E

Website	
Username	
Password	
Notes	

Website	
Username	
Password	
Notes	

Website	
Username	
Password	
Notes	

-E-

Website	
Username	
Password	
Notes	

Website	
Username	
Password	
Notes	

Website	
Username	
Password	
Notes	

-E-

Website	
Username	
Password	
Notes	

Website	
Username	
Password	
Notes	

Website	
Username	
Password	
Notes	

Website	
Username	
Password	
Notes	
Website	
Username	
Password	
Notes	
Website	
Username	
Password	
Notes	

-F-

Website	
Username	
Password	
Notes	

Website	
Username	
Password	
Notes	

Website	
Username	
Password	
Notes	

Website	
Username	
Password	
Notes	
Website	
Username	
Password	
Notes	
Website	
Username	
Password	
Notes	

F

Website	
Username	
Password	
Notes	

Website	
Username	
Password	
Notes	

Website	
Username	
Password	
Notes	

-F-

Website	
Username	
Password	
Notes	

Website	
Username	
Password	
Notes	

Website	
Username	
Password	
Notes	

-F-

Website	
Username	
Password	
Notes	

Website	
Username	
Password	
Notes	

Website	
Username	
Password	
Notes	

Website	
Username	
Password	
Notes	

Website	
Username	
Password	
Notes	

Website	
Username	
Password	
Notes	

-G-

Website	
Username	
Password	
Notes	

Website	
Username	
Password	
Notes	

Website	
Username	
Password	
Notes	

Website	
Username	
Password	
Notes	

Website	
Username	
Password	
Notes	

Website	
Username	
Password	
Notes	

-G-

Website	
Username	
Password	
Notes	

Website	
Username	
Password	
Notes	

Website	
Username	
Password	
Notes	

Website	
Username	
Password	
Notes	

Website	
Username	
Password	
Notes	

Website	
Username	
Password	
Notes	

-H-

Website	
Username	
Password	
Notes	

Website	
Username	
Password	
Notes	

Website	
Username	
Password	
Notes	

-H-

Website	
Username	
Password	
Notes	

Website	
Username	
Password	
Notes	

Website	
Username	
Password	
Notes	

-H-

Website	
Username	
Password	
Notes	

Website	
Username	
Password	
Notes	

Website	
Username	
Password	
Notes	

-H-

Website	
Username	
Password	
Notes	

Website	
Username	
Password	
Notes	

Website	
Username	
Password	
Notes	

-H-

Website	
Username	
Password	
Notes	

Website	
Username	
Password	
Notes	

Website	
Username	
Password	
Notes	

Website	
Username	
Password	
Notes	

Website	
Username	
Password	
Notes	

Website	
Username	
Password	
Notes	

-I-

Website	
Username	
Password	
Notes	

Website	
Username	
Password	
Notes	

Website	
Username	
Password	
Notes	

Website	
Username	
Password	
Notes	

Website	
Username	
Password	
Notes	

Website	
Username	
Password	
Notes	

-I-

Website	
Username	
Password	
Notes	

Website	
Username	
Password	
Notes	

Website	
Username	
Password	
Notes	

Website	
Username	
Password	
Notes	

Website	
Username	
Password	
Notes	

Website	
Username	
Password	
Notes	

-J-

Website	
Username	
Password	
Notes	

Website	
Username	
Password	
Notes	

Website	
Username	
Password	
Notes	

-J-

Website	
Username	
Password	
Notes	

Website	
Username	
Password	
Notes	

Website	
Username	
Password	
Notes	

-J-

Website	
Username	
Password	
Notes	

Website	
Username	
Password	
Notes	

Website	
Username	
Password	
Notes	

Website	
Username	
Password	
Notes	

Website	
Username	
Password	
Notes	

Website	
Username	
Password	
Notes	

Website	
Username	
Password	
Notes		

Website	
Username	
Password	
Notes		

Website	
Username	
Password	
Notes		

Website	
Username	
Password	
Notes	

Website	
Username	
Password	
Notes	

Website	
Username	
Password	
Notes	

Website	
Username	
Password	
Notes	

Website	
Username	
Password	
Notes	

Website	
Username	
Password	
Notes	

Website	
Username	
Password	
Notes	

Website	
Username	
Password	
Notes	

Website	
Username	
Password	
Notes	

Website	
Username	
Password	
Notes	

Website	
Username	
Password	
Notes	

Website	
Username	
Password	
Notes	

Website	
Username	
Password	
Notes	

Website	
Username	
Password	
Notes	

Website	
Username	
Password	
Notes	

-L-

Website	
Username	
Password	
Notes	

Website	
Username	
Password	
Notes	

Website	
Username	
Password	
Notes	

Website	
Username	
Password	
Notes	

Website	
Username	
Password	
Notes	

Website	
Username	
Password	
Notes	

-L-

Website	
Username	
Password	
Notes	

Website	
Username	
Password	
Notes	

Website	
Username	
Password	
Notes	

L

Website	
Username	
Password	
Notes	

Website	
Username	
Password	
Notes	

Website	
Username	
Password	
Notes	

-L-

Website	
Username	
Password	
Notes	

Website	
Username	
Password	
Notes	

Website	
Username	
Password	
Notes	

Website	
Username	
Password	
Notes	

Website	
Username	
Password	
Notes	

Website	
Username	
Password	
Notes	

Website	
Username	
Password	
Notes	

Website	
Username	
Password	
Notes	

Website	
Username	
Password	
Notes	

Website	
Username	
Password	
Notes	

Website	
Username	
Password	
Notes	

Website	
Username	
Password	
Notes	

Website	
Username	
Password	
Notes	

Website	
Username	
Password	
Notes	

Website	
Username	
Password	
Notes	

Website	
Username	
Password	
Notes	

Website	
Username	
Password	
Notes	

Website	
Username	
Password	
Notes	

-N-

Website	
Username	
Password	
Notes	

Website	
Username	
Password	
Notes	

Website	
Username	
Password	
Notes	

Website	
Username	
Password	
Notes	

Website	
Username	
Password	
Notes	

Website	
Username	
Password	
Notes	

Website	
Username	
Password	
Notes	

Website	
Username	
Password	
Notes	

Website	
Username	
Password	
Notes	

Website	
Username	
Password	
Notes	

Website	
Username	
Password	
Notes	

Website	
Username	
Password	
Notes	

Website	
Username	
Password	
Notes	

Website	
Username	
Password	
Notes	

Website	
Username	
Password	
Notes	

Website	
Username	
Password	
Notes	

Website	
Username	
Password	
Notes	

Website	
Username	
Password	
Notes	

-O-

Website	
Username	
Password	
Notes	

Website	
Username	
Password	
Notes	

Website	
Username	
Password	
Notes	

Website	
Username	
Password	
Notes	

Website	
Username	
Password	
Notes	

Website	
Username	
Password	
Notes	

O

Website	
Username	
Password	
Notes	

Website	
Username	
Password	
Notes	

Website	
Username	
Password	
Notes	

Website	
Username	
Password	
Notes	
Website	
Username	
Password	
Notes	
Website	
Username	
Password	
Notes	

-P-

Website	
Username	
Password	
Notes	

Website	
Username	
Password	
Notes	

Website	
Username	
Password	
Notes	

-P-

Website	
Username	
Password	
Notes	

Website	
Username	
Password	
Notes	

Website	
Username	
Password	
Notes	

-P-

Website	
Username	
Password	
Notes	

Website	
Username	
Password	
Notes	

Website	
Username	
Password	
Notes	

-P-

Website	
Username	
Password	
Notes	

Website	
Username	
Password	
Notes	

Website	
Username	
Password	
Notes	

-P-

Website	
Username	
Password	
Notes	

Website	
Username	
Password	
Notes	

Website	
Username	
Password	
Notes	

Website	
Username	
Password	
Notes	

Website	
Username	
Password	
Notes	

Website	
Username	
Password	
Notes	

Website	
Username	
Password	
Notes	

Website	
Username	
Password	
Notes	

Website	
Username	
Password	
Notes	

Website	
Username	
Password	
Notes	

Website	
Username	
Password	
Notes	

Website	
Username	
Password	
Notes	

Website	
Username	
Password	
Notes	

Website	
Username	
Password	
Notes	

Website	
Username	
Password	
Notes	

Website	
Username	
Password	
Notes	

Website	
Username	
Password	
Notes	

Website	
Username	
Password	
Notes	

-R-

Website	
Username	
Password	
Notes	

Website	
Username	
Password	
Notes	

Website	
Username	
Password	
Notes	

Website	
Username	
Password	
Notes	

Website	
Username	
Password	
Notes	

Website	
Username	
Password	
Notes	

-R-

Website	
Username	
Password	
Notes	

Website	
Username	
Password	
Notes	

Website	
Username	
Password	
Notes	

-R-

Website	
Username	
Password	
Notes	

Website	
Username	
Password	
Notes	

Website	
Username	
Password	
Notes	

-R-

Website	
Username	
Password	
Notes	

Website	
Username	
Password	
Notes	

Website	
Username	
Password	
Notes	

Website	
Username	
Password	
Notes	

Website	
Username	
Password	
Notes	

Website	
Username	
Password	
Notes	

Website	
Username	
Password	
Notes	

Website	
Username	
Password	
Notes	

Website	
Username	
Password	
Notes	

Website	
Username	
Password	
Notes	

Website	
Username	
Password	
Notes	

Website	
Username	
Password	
Notes	

Website	
Username	
Password	
Notes	

Website	
Username	
Password	
Notes	

Website	
Username	
Password	
Notes	

Website	
Username	
Password	
Notes	

Website	
Username	
Password	
Notes	

Website	
Username	
Password	
Notes	

Website	
Username	
Password	
Notes	

Website	
Username	
Password	
Notes	

Website	
Username	
Password	
Notes	

Website	
Username	
Password	
Notes	

Website	
Username	
Password	
Notes	

Website	
Username	
Password	
Notes	

Website	
Username	
Password	
Notes	

Website	
Username	
Password	
Notes	

Website	
Username	
Password	
Notes	

Website	
Username	
Password	
Notes	

Website	
Username	
Password	
Notes	

Website	
Username	
Password	
Notes	

T

Website	
Username	
Password	
Notes	

Website	
Username	
Password	
Notes	

Website	
Username	
Password	
Notes	

Website	
Username	
Password	
Notes	
Website	
Username	
Password	
Notes	
Website	
Username	
Password	
Notes	

-U-

Website	
Username	
Password	
Notes	

Website	
Username	
Password	
Notes	

Website	
Username	
Password	
Notes	

Website	
Username	
Password	
Notes	

Website	
Username	
Password	
Notes	

Website	
Username	
Password	
Notes	

-U-

Website	
Username	
Password	
Notes	

Website	
Username	
Password	
Notes	

Website	
Username	
Password	
Notes	

Website	
Username	
Password	
Notes	

Website	
Username	
Password	
Notes	

Website	
Username	
Password	
Notes	

Website	
Username	
Password	
Notes	

Website	
Username	
Password	
Notes	

Website	
Username	
Password	
Notes	

Website	
Username	
Password	
Notes	

Website	
Username	
Password	
Notes	

Website	
Username	
Password	
Notes	

Website	
Username	
Password	
Notes	

Website	
Username	
Password	
Notes	

Website	
Username	
Password	
Notes	

Website	
Username	
Password	
Notes	

Website	
Username	
Password	
Notes	

Website	
Username	
Password	
Notes	

Website	
Username	
Password	
Notes	

Website	
Username	
Password	
Notes	

Website	
Username	
Password	
Notes	

Website	
Username	
Password	
Notes	

Website	
Username	
Password	
Notes	

Website	
Username	
Password	
Notes	

Website	
Username	
Password	
Notes	

Website	
Username	
Password	
Notes	

Website	
Username	
Password	
Notes	

Website	
Username	
Password	
Notes	

Website	
Username	
Password	
Notes	

Website	
Username	
Password	
Notes	

Website	
Username	
Password	
Notes	

Website	
Username	
Password	
Notes	

Website	
Username	
Password	
Notes	

Website	
Username	
Password	
Notes	

Website	
Username	
Password	
Notes	

Website	
Username	
Password	
Notes	

Website	
Username	
Password	
Notes	

Website	
Username	
Password	
Notes	

Website	
Username	
Password	
Notes	

Website	
Username	
Password	
Notes	

Website	
Username	
Password	
Notes	

Website	
Username	
Password	
Notes	

Website	
Username	
Password	
Notes	

Website	
Username	
Password	
Notes	

Website	
Username	
Password	
Notes	

Website	
Username	
Password	
Notes	

Website	
Username	
Password	
Notes	

Website	
Username	
Password	
Notes	

Website	
Username	
Password	
Notes	

Website	
Username	
Password	
Notes	

Website	
Username	
Password	
Notes	

Website	
Username	
Password	
Notes	

Website	
Username	
Password	
Notes	

Website	
Username	
Password	
Notes	

Website	
Username	
Password	
Notes	

Website	
Username	
Password	
Notes	

Website	
Username	
Password	
Notes	

Website	
Username	
Password	
Notes	

Website	
Username	
Password	
Notes	

Website	
Username	
Password	
Notes	

Website	
Username	
Password	
Notes	

Website	
Username	
Password	
Notes	

Website	
Username	
Password	
Notes	

Website	
Username	
Password	
Notes	

Website	
Username	
Password	
Notes	

Website	
Username	
Password	
Notes	

-Z-

Website	
Username	
Password	
Notes	

Website	
Username	
Password	
Notes	

Website	
Username	
Password	
Notes	

-Z-

Website	
Username	
Password	
Notes	

Website	
Username	
Password	
Notes	

Website	
Username	
Password	
Notes	

Website	
Username	
Password	
Notes	

Website	
Username	
Password	
Notes	

Website	
Username	
Password	
Notes	

-Z-

Website	
Username	
Password	
Notes	

Website	
Username	
Password	
Notes	

Website	
Username	
Password	
Notes	

-Z-

Website	
Username	
Password	
Notes	

Website	
Username	
Password	
Notes	

Website	
Username	
Password	
Notes	

Notes

www.ingramcontent.com/pod-product-compliance
Lightning Source LLC
Chambersburg PA
CBHW070232180526
45158CB00001BA/454